WITHDRAWN

Taste Something New!
Giving Different Foods a Try

Jennifer Boothroyd

Lerner Publications • Minneapolis

For Gerry, my foodie friend

Note from the editor: This book includes some meal and snack ideas that kids might like to try, but please note that for health and safety reasons, children should always get permission from a parent or a guardian before trying any new food.

Lerner Publications Company
A division of Lerner Publishing Group, Inc.
241 First Avenue North
Minneapolis, MN 55401 USA

For reading levels and more information, look up this title at www.lernerbooks.com.

Library of Congress Cataloging-in-Publication Data

Boothroyd, Jennifer, 1972– author.
    Taste something new : giving different foods a try / Jennifer Boothroyd.
        pages cm. — (Lightning bolt books. Healthy eating)
    Audience: Ages 5–8.
    Audience: K to grade 3.
    Includes bibliographical references and index.
        ISBN 978-1-4677-9472-5 (lb : alk. paper) — ISBN 978-1-4677-9675-0 (pb : alk. paper) —
ISBN 978-1-4677-9676-7 (eb pdf)
        1. Dietetics—Juvenile literature. 2. Nutrition—Juvenile literature. 3. Health—Juvenile
literature. 4. Cooking—Juvenile literature. I. Title.
    RM216.B685 2016
    613.2083—dc23   2015015210

Manufactured in the United States of America
1 – BP – 12/31/15

Table of Contents

A Variety of Foods

Look at all these fruits and vegetables! You probably know many of them. But how many have you tried?

We get nutrients from food. **Nutrients keep our bodies healthy.**

Healthy bodies have energy to play!

5

It's important to eat a variety of foods. That way, you get many different nutrients.

Different foods give you different nutrients.

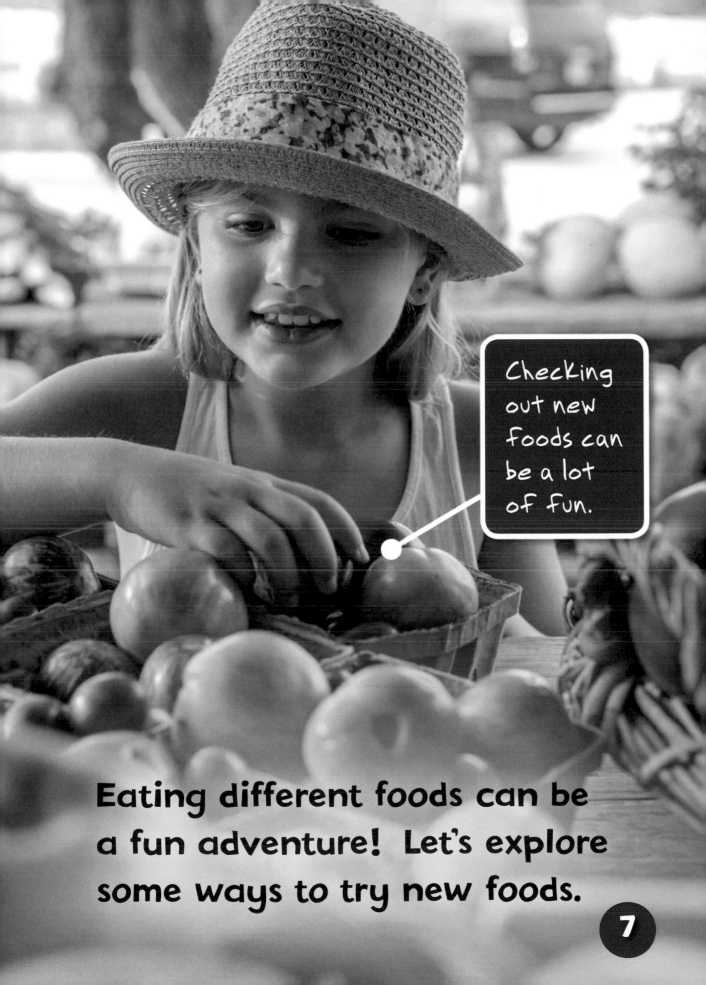

Eating different foods can be a fun adventure! Let's explore some ways to try new foods.

Fresh, Frozen, or Canned

Stores sell food in many ways. How a food is stored can make a difference in how it tastes. Stores sell fresh, frozen, and canned pineapple.

Pineapple is a good source of vitamin C.

Eating fresh fruit salad lets you try many fruits.

Fresh food hasn't been cooked or frozen. It hasn't been stored in a can or a jar. Trying different fresh fruits and veggies helps you find the ones you like. Lots of people think fruits and veggies taste best fresh!

Frozen foods often must be thawed or heated before you can eat them.

Some foods are stored in a freezer. Most grocery stores have a frozen food aisle. Try frozen peas or squash. Frozen berries are great for making smoothies!

Some foods have been canned. These foods are in cans or jars. Canned beans are yummy in salsa. Applesauce from a jar makes a tasty snack.

Black beans are packed with protein and fiber.

Some of these green beans are fresh. Some are frozen. Some are canned. Can you see a difference?

Try to eat a mix of fresh, frozen, and canned foods. See which ones you like!

Raw or Cooked

How a food is prepared can make a difference in how it tastes. It can also change a food's texture.

There are many different ways to cook food. Many foods can be baked or roasted in an oven. Maybe you'd like to try a baked potato. What about a roasted pear?

Baked potatoes are a tasty way to get potassium and vitamin C.

This pasta is almost ready to eat!

Some foods are cooked in a pan. Some are boiled in a pot of water. Have you tasted eggs from a frying pan? Or pasta that's been boiled on a stove?

Some foods can be eaten without cooking. Raw foods are uncooked. Would you like to try a raw carrot? Raw celery is yummy with peanut butter and raisins!

Raw veggies can be fun to try!

Raw vegetables are usually crunchier than cooked ones.

17

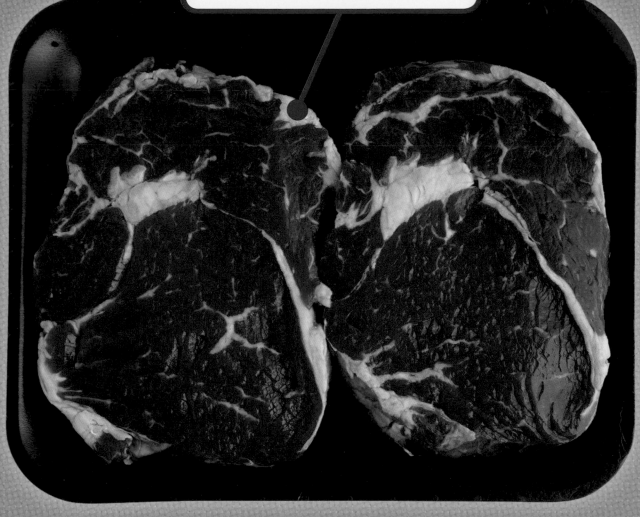

Some foods should not be eaten raw. They can make you sick.

Starting a Food Adventure

Are you looking for more ways to try new foods?

Exploring a grocery store can help you find new foods.

Talk to your friends. Ask them about foods they like to eat.

Your friends may like foods you haven't tried before.

Farmers' markets sell a variety of healthy foods.

Visit a farmers' market. Here farmers sell food they have grown.

Try growing your own fruits or vegetables. Food you grow yourself will be the freshest you can get.

If you don't have space outside for a garden, you can grow many plants in small containers.

Making food from scratch can be fun!

Ask an adult if you can help make a meal for your family. You can choose the ingredients and learn how to prepare the food.

Try foods from different countries. You may have eaten chicken, but have you tried teriyaki chicken? What about chicken enchiladas or chicken Parmesan?

Many people like chicken enchiladas.

Food adventures aren't always perfect. Sometimes you'll try a food you don't like. But you don't have to give up on that food forever!

Try the food in different ways. Try it cooked. Try it raw. Try it fresh or from a can. You may find you like it!

Trying different foods can help you find a new favorite.

Try This!

Ask an adult to help you plan a taste test for your family. Pick a food most of you have never eaten. Prepare the food in at least two different ways. Have everyone try a little of each. Talk about which ones you liked and which ones you didn't. Here are a couple of ideas to get you started:

- Try sliced raw kiwi and kiwi in a smoothie.

- Try raw cauliflower with or without dip. Cook frozen cauliflower and serve it with cheese on top. Follow a recipe for mashed cauliflower.

Fun Facts

- Chickpeas can be eaten in many ways. You can add some to a salad. You can put them in a soup. You can even mash them to make a spread called hummus!

- You have probably eaten a banana. But have you ever tried a plantain? Plantains are bigger than bananas, and most people don't eat them raw. Instead, people bake, fry, or grill the fruit.

- Grocery stores sell different kinds of milk. Cow's milk is one kind. Most stores also carry soy milk, almond milk, coconut milk, and rice milk.

Glossary

boiled: cooked in bubbling, steaming water

canned: stored in a can or jar

ingredient: the food used in a recipe

nutrient: something plants and animals need to live and grow

raw: uncooked

texture: the look and feel of something

Further Reading

Bellisario, Gina. *Choose Good Food! My Eating Tips.* Minneapolis: Millbrook Press, 2014.

KidsHealth: Recipes and Cooking
http://kidshealth.org/kid/recipes

Kids in the Kitchen
http://www.nutrition.gov/life-stages/children/kids-kitchen

Larson, Jennifer S. *Yummy Soup and Salad Recipes.* Minneapolis: Millbrook Press, 2013.

MyPlate Kids' Place
http://www.choosemyplate.gov/kids

Index

Photo Acknowledgments

The images in this book are used with the permission of: © SOMMAI/Shutterstock.com, p. 2; © iStockphoto.com/deyangeorgiev, p. 4; © Sergey Novikov/Shutterstock.com, p. 5; © iStockphoto.com/mediaphotos, p. 6; © Mark Edward Atkinson/Tracey Lee/Blend Images/Getty Images, p. 7; © Sergiy Kuzmin/Shutterstock.com, p. 8; © Tim Pannell/CORBIS, p. 9; © Ashlae W/Getty Images, p. 10; © Gayvoronskaya_Yana/Shutterstock.com, p. 11; © iStockphoto.com/marcociannarel, p. 12 (top); © iStockphoto.com/Savany, p. 12 (middle); © iStockphoto.com/ncognet0, p. 12 (bottom); © Monkey Business Images/Shutterstock.com, p. 13; © RoJo Images/Shutterstock.com, p. 14; © iStockphoto.com/tomasworks, p. 15; © Robyn Mackenzie/Shutterstock.com, p. 16; © KidStock/Blend Images/Getty Images, pp. 17, 27; © Paul Cowan/Shutterstock.com, p. 18; © Andersen Ross/Getty Images, p. 19; © Tetra Images/Jamie Grill/Getty Images, p. 20; © Peathegee Inc/Getty Images, p. 21; © Ariel Skelley/Brand X Pictures/Getty Images, p. 22; © Federico Candoni/Alamy, p. 23; © Ariel Skelley/Blend Images/Getty Images, p. 24; © iStockphoto.com/JoeGough, p. 25; © altrendo images/Getty Images, p. 26; © Hinterhaus Productions/Getty Images, p. 28; © Alexandralaw1977/Shutterstock.com, p. 30.

Front cover: © iStockphoto.com/desnik.

Main body text set in Johann Light 30/36.